WITHDRAWN

Vicente Fox

A Proud Heritage The Hispanic Library

Vicente Fox

The Road to the Mexican Presidency

Ann Gaines

The Child's World

Published in the United States of America by The Child's World®
PO Box 326 • Chanhassen, MN 55317-0326 • 800-599-READ • www.childsworld.com

Acknowledgments

The Creative Spark: Mary Francis-DeMarois, Project Director; Carrie Nichols Cantor, Series Editor; Robert Court, Design and Art Direction
Carmen Blanco, Curriculum Adviser
The Child's World®: Mary Berendes, Publishing Director

Photos

AFP/CORBIS: 23, 27, 28, 31; AP/Wide World Photos: 29; Carrie Nichols Cantor: 9; Sergio Dorantes/CORBIS: 24; Randy Faris/CORBIS: 8; Stephen Ferry/Getty Images: 14; Hulton Archive/Getty Images: 7, 33; Jeffry W. Myers/CORBIS: 18; Reuters NewMedia Inc./CORBIS: cover, 13, 30, 32, 34; Galen Rowell/CORBIS: 11; Phil Schermeister/CORBIS: 17

Library of Congress Cataloging-in-Publication Data
Gaines, Ann.
Vicente Fox : the road to the Mexican presidency / by Ann Gaines.
p. cm. — (A proud heritage : the hispanic library series)
Includes bibliographical references and index.
ISBN 1-56766-177-7 (lib. bdg. : alk. paper)
1. Fox Quesada, Vicente—Juvenile literature. 2. Mexico—Politics and government—1988—Juvenile literature. 3. Presidents—Mexico—Biography—Juvenile literature. I. Title. II. Proud heritage (Child's World (Firm))
F1236.6.F69G35 2003
972.08'41'092—dc21
[B]
2002151728

Chapter One

Beginnings

On July 2, 2000, his 58th birthday, Vicente Fox was elected president of Mexico. His amazing victory made headlines around the world. A few years earlier, no one would have predicted this successful businessman would one day make it to Los Piños, the Mexican White House.

In fact, until 1993, Vicente Fox could not even think of running for president. Before that time, Mexican law said that, in order to be eligible for the office, a **candidate** had to have Mexican-born parents. Vicente Fox's father, José Luis Fox, was indeed a native of Mexico. But his mother, Mercedes Quesada, was an **immigrant,** born in Spain. Her family had come to Mexico when she was a baby. Luckily for Fox, this law was changed, and he was able to become a presidential candidate.

Vicente Fox was born on July 2, 1942, in Mexico City. He was given the formal name Vicente Fox Quesada.

Vicente Fox was elected president of Mexico on July 2, 2000.

It is traditional among Mexicans of Spanish heritage to give babies a surname that combines both parents' surnames.

Growing Up on a Ranch

At the time of Vicente's birth, José Luis Fox and Mercedes Quesada had been married only a few years. They had one other child, a son. Like many young people, they

Vicente Fox was born in Mexico City. It is one of the largest cities in the world.

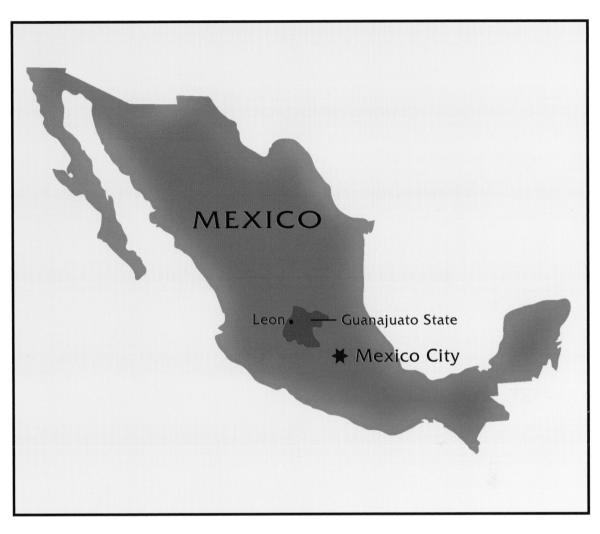

Vicente Fox grew up on a ranch in the state of Guanajuato.

possessed high hopes for the future. They did not want to raise their family in Mexico City, one of the largest cities on earth. They thought it would be healthier for their children to live in the country. While Vicente was still a baby, they moved to the state of Guanajuato, in the central part of the country. Guanajuato is a beautiful area with many mountains. Centuries ago, after silver was discovered there, many mines were opened.

The Foxes moved to Guanajuato because they had inherited a ranch from José Luis Fox's father near the small town San Francisco del Rincon. Léon, the nearest city, was a long drive away. The ranch, called San Cristobal, was very old. It was part of a huge **hacienda** established in 1591 by one of the Spaniards who came to Mexico to conquer its natives and claim their land for Spain. José Luis Fox's father, who had been born in Ireland, had moved to Mexico and purchased the ranch around 1911 during the Mexican Revolution.

The Fox family owned 1,100 acres (446 hectares). But Guanajuato gets little rain. The Foxes had to work hard in order to make the ranch productive. At first they used their land mainly to raise cattle. Later they also began to grow vegetables. Many other families of farm workers lived on the ranch as well.

Over time the Fox family grew to include nine children. They were a close family. When they were small, their mother taught them their letters and numbers. As they grew bigger, they spent more time with their father, working by his side. They grew up riding horses and tending cattle. Vicente liked to dream that he would grow up to become a bullfighter.

In their free time, the Fox brothers and sisters played together. They had many friends, including the ranch workers' children, who often came to their house to eat. Most Sundays the Fox family went to church together. Vicente Fox was raised as a Catholic. He was an altar boy. Every year, he participated in *posadas* and other church celebrations. A posada is a procession made by Catholic children during the Christmas season. They dress

Guanajuato is dry but very beautiful. The Foxes had to work hard to make a living on their ranch.

up as Mary and Joseph and go from house to house, pretending to seek shelter for the night.

Seeing His Countrymen's Struggles

In the 1940s, many Mexican children went to school for only a few years, if at all. Millions of children had to work their entire lives to help support their families. The Fox family lived quite comfortably, however. Vicente's parents insisted that all their children receive a good education. They sent them to a nearby school run by **Jesuit** priests. To get to school, Vicente and his brothers and sisters rode on horseback and in a small truck.

Vicente always did well in school, excelling in math. One year his parents sent him to the United States to a private high school in Prairie du Chien, Wisconsin, to learn English. He returned home speaking fluent, although accented, English.

By age 18 Vicente Fox stood six feet, six inches (200 centimeters) tall. Used to working outdoors, he was slender but strong. He loved to talk, joke, and tell stories, and he made friends easily.

Vicente Fox looks back on his youth fondly. His was a happy family that never went without. They always had plenty to eat and a nice house. He especially appreciated the things they had because every day he saw families

Vicente Fox was able to give his children an easier life than he had. In this photograph, he walks with his son Rodrigo and U.S. president George W. Bush.

struggling to get by. He grew up understanding, in his own words, "my country's painful inequalities." While his own childhood was happy, Vicente Fox learned that not everybody has an easy life.

Economists call the United States and some other nations, like Great Britain and Japan, developed nations. This means that they have a great deal of industry and wealth. Their many factories produce goods that they sell both at home and around the world. But Mexico's **economy,** like that of most countries, is less developed. It does not have much industry.

The lack of industry means many people don't have jobs. The jobs that exist generally do not pay well. As a result, there are millions of poor people in Mexico.

Living in poverty does not necessarily mean their lives are unhappy. But Mexico's poor people encounter many serious problems in their everyday lives. Many families cannot afford to eat well or see a doctor or dentist regularly. Many children also have to leave school after only a few years to go to work to help support their families.

Chapter Two

Out on His Own

After Vicente Fox finished high school, he went to the Universidad Iberoamericana, a Jesuit university in Mexico City. He loved the city's world-class museums and exciting nightlife. He spent his days listening to lectures in his classes, most of which were related to business. At the library he researched and wrote long papers. Schoolwork had always come easily to him, and he liked it well enough. Fox later said that at the university he gained important skills, such as how to analyze information.

What he enjoyed most about attending the university was the people he met. He formed friendships that lasted for years. He and his classmates had some of the brightest minds in Mexico. Like so many students, they spent a lot of time engaged in long conversations, arguing over the issues of the day.

At age 22, Fox left the university. Although he had completed his classwork, he did not take the final exam and thus received no diploma. He didn't take that exam until more than 30 years later!

A Career Selling Soda

In the meantime, Fox went to work for Coca-Cola de México, Inc., one of the largest companies in the country. Coca-Cola managers wanted him to start working in an office. Although Fox hoped one day to become a business executive, he asked to start in a different sort of position. He chose to be a deliveryman.

Fox drove a truck route that took him all across the central state of Michoacan. The job had long hours and required a lot of heavy lifting. Fox, however, was used to hard work. He liked learning about the company from the workers' point of view. One of his responsibilities was taking orders from storeowners and shopkeepers. He discovered he was a natural salesman who was able to persuade people to buy more and more of his company's product.

Fox's superiors were impressed with his willingness to work and his good business sense. He soon began to receive promotions. He became an executive and took on more responsibilities.

Looking back, Fox says one reason he succeeded at Coca-Cola was because of the time he had spent just selling Cokes. "I learned that the heart of a business is out in the field, not in the office," Fox once said. His rise in the Coca-Cola company continued for the next ten years.

Coca-Cola

Coca-Cola is an extremely popular drink in Mexico. The country buys more cokes per person than any other country in the world, including the United States.

Many American tourists who visit Mexico say ice-cold Coca-Cola seems to taste especially delicious in that hot land. In fact, the recipe used by many Mexican bottlers is slightly different from the one used in the United States.

Coca-Cola seems to be everywhere in Mexico. It is sold by supermarkets and many neighborhood grocery shops. Tiny taco stands offer only Cokes to drink. Travelers driving across the deserts count on finding Coca-Cola at every gas station. As a result of the popularity of Cokes, Coca-Cola de México is one of the country's biggest and most profitable companies.

The Mexican currency is the peso (PAY-so).

By 1971, Vicente Fox was a successful and high-ranking executive at Coca-Cola. Other managers admired his planning ability. Yet his greatest strength lay in his ability to form working relationships with his employees. He made a point of meeting as many people in the company as possible. He encouraged employees to share their problems on the job with him. He found ways to make their work easier and more enjoyable.

At the same time, Fox was building his own family. After he and his secretary, Lillian de la Concha, married in 1971, they adopted four children. Their two daughters are named Ana Cristina and Paulina, and their two sons are named Vicente and Rodrigo. For a long time, theirs was a happy family. (Over time, however, the couple grew apart and divorced in 1991.)

In 1974, Fox became president of Coca-Cola de México. Despite his youth—he was only 32—he did very well in that demanding job. But there was one aspect of the job that he did not like. Coca-Cola, like all big **corporations,** sometimes had to work with Mexico's government. Years later he would remember feeling angry when the president of Mexico invited Fox and other businessmen to meetings to discuss Mexico's economic problems. He explained that he thought those meetings were a waste of time—that the president paid no attention to the suggestions he and his fellow businessmen made.

After just five years, in 1979, the international Coca-Cola company asked Fox to run all the branches of Coca-Cola in Latin America. Of course, Fox was very flattered by the offer. After serious consideration, he realized he did not want the job. He knew that if he took it he would no longer have much contact with company employees. Also taking the job would have required him and his family to move to Coca-Cola's international headquarters in the United States. He decided to leave the company.

At age 37, Vicente Fox went into business with his brothers. Together they owned and ran a company called Grupo Fox. Grupo Fox was a tiny business compared to Coca-Cola de México. It ran the ranch the Fox family still owned in Guanajuato. Another part of the business was a boot factory. Now Vicente Fox learned about *small* businesses. He came into contact with a new group of people very much like him.

The 1980s was a particularly hard time for small-business owners. Grupo Fox suffered a little less than other companies of its size because it sold a lot of vegetables in the United States. Nevertheless, Vicente Fox began to think more and more about the Mexican economy and its problems. He realized that small-business owners, especially, needed help from the Mexican government if their companies were to grow and create more jobs for the Mexican people. As time went by, Fox became interested in helping his country solve some of its economic problems. He decided he would do so by entering politics.

Chapter Three

Into Politics

Mexico is a **democracy.** Its people elect their leaders, including their president, members of **Congress,** state governors, and city mayors. But the system did not work the way it was supposed to. One **political party** dominated Mexican politics. The PRI—Partido Revolucionario Institucional, or the Institutional Revolutionary Party—had been established during the Mexican Revolution. From 1929 on, every single Mexican president belonged to the PRI. Almost every member of Congress also belonged to the PRI. Governors were always members of the PRI. Only a few people controlled the PRI. They decided who would run for office.

There were other serious problems with the PRI. Over the years the party had become **corrupt.** Some of its members accepted bribes. They took money from dishonest people in exchange for their vote. The PRI also cheated by stuffing ballot boxes with fake votes in some elections. In general, the party did not let voters have a real say in running their country.

Of course, many Mexicans did not like this. Some thought nothing could be done about the PRI and accepted the way things were. But others fought back by forming opposition political parties. The PAN—the Partido Accion Nacional, or National Action Party—founded in 1939, was the most active of these. But it was very weak. Its candidates ran for political office, but they won no important elections.

The Opposition Grows Stronger

In the 1980s, the PRI's opponents started to grow stronger. They gained power. In 1988, a businessman named Manuel Clouthier ran for president on the PAN ticket. Clouthier was a friend of Vicente Fox's. He and other PAN leaders knew Fox was a smart businessman with many ideas about to how to improve their country. They also knew he got along well with most people. He had a talent for speaking in public and convincing others to accept his point of view. They thought he would make a good politician. Clouthier and others encouraged Fox to run for office. Excited by the idea, Fox agreed to become a candidate for Congress in 1988.

Vicente Fox won that election. As a member of the lower house in Mexico's Congress (the **Chamber of Deputies**), he **represented** the people of the city of Léon. He did a good job in office. He spoke out against the president of Mexico. This earned him enemies in the PRI. But many of the people who had elected him thought he understood them and worked hard for them.

In 1990, Fox's term ended. The next year, Fox ran for governor of the state of Guanajuato. Many people

From 1988 to 1990, Vicente Fox represented the city of Léon in Mexico's Chamber of Deputies in Mexico City.

Fox ran for governor of the state of Guanajuato in 1991, but he lost.

thought he was going to win, but he lost. A member of the PRI won instead. Later everybody found out that the PRI had cheated in order to win. In some voting districts, more PRI votes were counted than there were voters. People from different political parties met and chose a new governor to finish out the term.

When the next election was held, in 1995, Fox ran again. This time he won by a landslide. He made a successful and popular governor. He helped the people of his state in many different ways. Farmers and ranchers liked him because he understood their problems. But the people who lived in Guanajuato cities, especially business owners, liked him too. When General Motors (GM) built a big new car factory in the state, it created many jobs. While this made Fox happy, he did not like the fact that the plant imported almost all its materials from the United States. Fox helped GM find suppliers in Mexico. This helped many small Mexican businesses.

Another thing Fox did as governor was to improve Guanajuato's public school system.

Going All the Way

Fox enjoyed his new job and was proud of his accomplishments in office. Nevertheless, he decided he would not run for governor again. He had set his sights even higher. In 1998, Vicente Fox announced he would run in the next presidential election. It was scheduled for the year 2000. His announcement created an uproar. No one had ever announced a candidacy so early.

Fox's move created trouble for the PRI. In the past, a few members of the PRI had always decided who would be the party's next candidate. Now many more of its members wanted a say in who would run. The party was forced to hold a **primary election** to allow its members to vote on who should run for president. Even after it selected a candidate, the PRI did not unite behind him.

The disarray of the PRI helped Vicente Fox. Thanks to his many years of business experience, he ran a well-organized campaign. He was able to raise a lot of money. Many volunteers turned out to help him. He was also aided by a **coalition** of PAN and another political party, the Mexican Green Party.

Chapter Four

President Fox

Over the next two years, as his presidential campaign progressed, Vicente Fox became very famous. He became a household name. As they became familiar with him, more and more people decided to vote for him.

Fox appealed to voters for many different reasons. One was the way he looked. On the campaign trail, he wore casual clothes, such as denim shirts and cowboy boots. His look helped ordinary people feel more comfortable with him than his opponent. In the past, the PAN had been seen as a party that was not very interested in helping poor people. But PAN had changed. It came to focus more on the problems of ordinary people. Many people also liked Fox's energetic personality. He held many political rallies. He encouraged the crowds to shout with him, *"Cambio!"* ("Change!").

Fox traveled all over Mexico to talk to people and convince them to vote for him.

Fox was a good campaigner. He made people feel they could relate to him. The colorful hat he is wearing is from the Chiapas region of Mexico.

People often liked the speeches Fox gave at rallies and on television. A gifted public speaker, he became excited when he talked about his vision of Mexico's future. He promised to fight political corruption, to **reform** the country's political system, and to create new social programs for the country's poor. He wanted every Mexican child to receive a good education. He said Mexico needed to build new factories and create new jobs. He also spoke at great length about persuading the United States to open its border with Mexico to let more Mexicans work there legally.

The United States and Mexico share one of the longest borders in the world. It stretches for 2,000 miles (3,300 kilometers). Laws dictate who can cross the borders.

Mexicans can easily enter the United States if they are going for a very short time. Many Mexicans who live just south of the border frequently cross to the other side to visit friends or shop, for example. But the United States strictly limits the number of Mexicans who can come there to work.

Officers employed by the Immigration and Naturalization Service (INS) patrol the border to prevent Mexicans from coming into the United States illegally. But many need the money they can make in the United States so badly they try to sneak across the border. Sometimes this ends in tragedy, as when people drown trying to cross the wide river called the Rio Grande that separates Texas and Mexico. Each of the white crosses in the picture above stands for one person who died trying to cross the border.

When Fox took over the presidency from Ernesto Zedillo, it was the first peaceful transfer of power in Mexican history.

And the Winner Is . . .

The election interested many people. More than the usual number of Mexicans went to vote on election day on July 2, 2000. When all the votes were counted, Fox had received 15,988,740 votes. Francisco Labastida, the PRI candidate, got 13,576,385 votes. Fox had won!

When Vicente Fox's victory was announced, people in Mexico and elsewhere expressed surprise. The PRI had been in power longer than any other political party in any country on earth. Fox's achievement was tremendous.

After the election, journalists reported that Mexicans felt optimistic about the future. Poor Mexicans hoped Fox would help them. The middle and upper classes hoped he would keep his promises and help Mexican businesses grow and prosper.

Vicente Fox was **inaugurated** on December 1, 2000. His term was for six years, until 2006. As president he

Fox's victory gave a big boost to democracy in Mexico.

proved once again that he was willing to work. He put in long hours at the office. He remembered the promises he had made the voters. Fox immediately began to work on reforms. He came up with new ways for officials to make sure Mexico's elections were fair. He also began to try to make the Mexican economy stronger.

Fox married his second wife, Marta, on his birthday in 2001.

Fox met with U.S. president George W. Bush soon after Bush took office in 2001. Pictured here, from left to right, are Marta and Vicente Fox and Laura and George W. Bush.

On July 2, 2001, Fox married Marta Sahagún Jiménez, at Los Piños. This day was also his 59th birthday and the first anniversary of Fox's presidency.

The Border Issue

One of Fox's goals was to improve relations between Mexico and the United States. In 2001, George W. Bush, the new U.S. president, made his first official trip outside the United States. That trip was to Mexico, where Bush visited Fox at his family's ranch. News reporters said that the two men seemed to like each other very much. They were able to talk openly about Mexico's problems and about opening the border. Bush began to try to win support for the idea from other American politicians.

Vicente Fox had a promising beginning. But then problems arose. On September 11, 2001, the United States

A Mexican legislator held up this sign for President Fox. It says, in Spanish, "Where are the millions of jobs that were supposed to be created?"

was attacked by foreign terrorists. People in the United States became nervous about foreigners. Many wanted to close, not open, their nation's borders, which disappointed the Mexican people.

At the same time, Mexicans began to question whether Fox would be able to fulfill his other promises. Fox acknowledged that he was having more problems doing so than he had expected. Mexico, a country steeped in tradition, was slow to change. Yet Vicente Fox remains as determined as ever to achieve his goal of improving the lives of Mexicans.

In October 2002, Fox hosted a meeting in Mexico of the leaders of many nations in the Pacific Ocean, including the United States, Canada, Australia, China, Japan, Korea, and Peru. They gathered to talk about trade. Fox was happy when many of them expressed interest in trading with Mexico, since one of his greatest hopes is to help his country sell more of its goods around the world.

By 2003, Vicente Fox had served half of his elected term as president of Mexico. Although he has sometimes found it difficult to accomplish all he wants to do, he prides himself on the job he has done so far. He plans to continue to try to bring about positive change for his country, especially by strengthening the Mexican economy.

1942: Vicente Fox Quesada is born on July 2.

1960: Fox leaves home to go to Mexico City, where he enrolls in the Universidad Iberoamericana, a Jesuit university.

1964: Fox goes to work for Coca-Cola de México, one of the country's largest companies, as a salesman.

1971: Fox becomes an executive at Coca-Cola de México, with an office at corporate headquarters in Mexico City. He marries his secretary, Lillian de la Concha.

1974: Fox becomes president of Coca-Cola de México.

1979: The international Coca-Cola corporation asks Fox to take charge of all of their Latin American operations. He decides not to accept this offer, leaves the Coca-Cola company, and goes to work for his family's business, Grupo Fox.

1988: Fox runs for political office for the first time and wins election to the Chamber of Deputies, the lower house of Mexico's Congress.

1991: Fox runs for governor of the state of Guanajuato and is defeated.

1995: Fox runs for governor again and wins by a landslide.

1998: Fox begins campaigning to be president of Mexico.

2000: Fox is elected president on his birthday, July 2. He is inaugurated on December 1.

2001: In February, U.S. president George W. Bush takes his first official trip outside the United States, to Mexico. He visits Vicente Fox at Fox's ranch. The two men talk about the possibility of the United States opening its border to more Mexican workers. But discussions stall after September 11, when the United States is attacked by terrorists.

2002: In October, Fox hosts Asia-Pacific Economic Cooperation Forum, a conference of nations in the Pacific Ocean.

candidate (KAN-duh-date) A candidate is a person who runs for election to a political office. Voters cast their ballot for the candidate they like best.

Chamber of Deputies (CHAYM-ber uv DEP-yoo-teez) The Chamber of Deputies is one of two houses in the Mexican Congress. The Mexican Chamber of Deputies is similar to the United States House of Representatives.

coalition (koh-uh-LIH-shun) A coalition is a temporary joining together of two separate groups. Two political parties formed a coalition during the Mexican presidential election of 2000.

Congress (KONG-ress) In Mexico, as in the United States, Congress is the branch of the federal government that makes the laws of the nation. Members of Congress are elected.

corporations (kor-puh-RAY-shunz) A corporation is a legal company or business. Coca-Cola is one of the largest corporations in Mexico.

corrupt (kuh-RUPT) To be corrupt is to be dishonest or to use your position to enrich yourself rather than do the job you are supposed to do. A corrupt politician takes bribes or cheats to win elections.

democracy (deh-MOCK-ruh-see) A democracy is a government that is run by men and women elected by the people. In a democracy, voters cast ballots to select who will represent them in their government.

economy (ee-KON-uh-mee) The economy of a country has to do with how many jobs there are and how much buying and selling of products is taking place. In a strong economy, people buy and sell a lot of products, there are plenty of jobs, and lots of people earn good money.

hacienda (hah-see-EN-duh) A hacienda is a large farm owned by one family and worked on by many laborers. A hacienda is the Spanish version of a plantation.

immigrant (IH-muh-grent) An immigrant is a person who leaves the country where he or she was born and goes to live in a foreign country. Vicente Fox's mother was an immigrant from Spain.

inaugurated (ih-NAW-guh-ray-ted) To be inaugurated is to be sworn into office. Vicente Fox was inaugurated as president of Mexico on December 1, 2000.

Jesuit (JEH-zoo-it) A Jesuit is a member of a Catholic religious order called, in English, the Society of Jesus. Jesuits are noted especially for their education and teaching.

political party (puh-LIH-tih-kul PAR-tee) A political party is an organized group of people who share the same political views. Each political party nominates its own candidates to run for different offices, such as president or member of Congress.

primary election (PRY-meh-ree uh-LEK-shun) In a primary election, voters who are members of the same party vote to choose which one of several candidates will become that party's candidate to run in an election against the other party's candidate. After Vicente Fox declared his candidacy, the PRI held a primary election to decide who would run against him.

reform (ree-FORM) To reform something is to change it for the better. Vicente Fox promised the Mexican people he would reform their political system.

represented (reh-prih-ZEN-ted) When a group is represented by someone, that means the person acts and speaks for that group. As a member of Congress, Fox represented the people who elected him.

Books

Carew-Miller, Anna. *Famous People of Mexico*. New York: Mason Crest, 2002.

Hunter, Amy Nicole. *History of Mexico*. New York: Mason Crest, 2002.

Pascoe, Elaine. *Mexico and the United States: Conflict and Cooperation*. New York: Twenty-First Century Books, 1996.

Williams, Colleen. *The People of Mexico*. New York: Mason Crest, 2002.

Web Sites

Visit our Web page for lots of links about Vicente Fox:
http://www.childsworld.com/links.html

Note to parents, teachers, and librarians: We routinely monitor our Web links to make sure they're safe, active sites.

Sources Used by the Author

"Fox Quesada, Vicente," *Current Biography* (May 2001), pp. 45–51.

"Mexican Politics" Web page posted on The PBS Online News Hour Web site at *http://www.pbs.org/newshour/bb/latin_america/mexico_index.html*

"PAN," *www.pan.org.mx*

"Psychology of Power," on the Time.com Web site at *www.time.com/time/magazine/intl/article/0,9171,1107000529-47008,00.html*

"Vicente Fox," *Newsmakers,* Issue 1. Gale Group essay reproduced in *Biography Resource Center* (Farmington Hills, Mich.: Gale Group, 2001).

"Vicente Fox," Gale Group essay reproduced in *Biography Resource Center* (Farmington Hills, Mich.: Gale Group, 2001.) Available through the Biography Resource Center Online.

"Vicente Fox Is President-Elect for 2000–2006," Lloyd Mexican Economic Report, *August 2000, http://www.mexconnect.com/MEX/lloyds/llydeco0800.html*